Helen Orme is a successful author of fiction and non-fiction, particularly for reluctant and struggling readers. She has written over fifty books for Ransom Publishing.

Helen was a teacher for nearly thirty years. She worked as a Special Educational Needs Co-ordinator in a large comprehensive school, as an advisory teacher for IT and as teacher-in-charge for a pupil referral unit. These experiences have been invaluable in her writing.

StreetWise

The Best Thing Ever

gambling, rebelling against parents

Speed

getting involved in crime

The Newcomer

outsiders, racism, intolerance

I Dare You

taking risks

Fixed It!

cyberbullying

I Can't Help It

smoking

Best Mates

coping with peer pressure

Everyone Does It

cheating

Just Try It!

drugs

Don't Believe Her

sex

Just One More

alcohol

Taking Responsibility

conflicting priorities: home and school

Don't Believe Her

Helen Orme

StreetWise

Don't Believe Her
by Helen Orme

Published by Ransom Publishing Ltd.
Radley House, 8 St. Cross Road, Winchester, Hampshire SO23 9HX, UK
www.ransom.co.uk

ISBN 978 184167 356 1
First published in 2014

A CIP catalogue record of this book is available from the British Library.

CONTENTS

ONE

The Party

'Hey, wait for me.'

Alfie looked back. It was Jen.

'How's things?' he asked, as she caught up.

'Cool. You?'

'Not bad. It's Carrie's birthday on Saturday. Want to come to her party?'

'You sure?'

Jen knew that Carrie didn't really like her. Carrie was Alfie's girlfriend, but Jen was his best friend.

*****

The party, at Carrie's house, was better than she had thought.

There were some really nice guys: some of Alfie's friends and some she didn't know so well.

She was chatting with them when she heard a shout of laughter from Joe and Adam. She wanted to know what was going on.

'Back in a minute,' she said.

'What's the matter with you two?'

'Did you see?' asked Joe.

'See what?'

'Alfie and Carrie,' sniggered Adam. 'They've gone upstairs!'

'So?'

'Oh, come on. She's sixteen today, isn't she? It's legal now.'

Then he whispered something else to Joe. Jen was glad she hadn't heard what it was.

'Get a life, you two,' she said. 'Who

cares what they're doing?'

'You're just jealous,' said Adam. 'Want to try it with me?'

Jen turned her back on them.

She wouldn't show those two she cared.

TWO

I Need to Talk

On Monday Jen left home a bit later. She didn't want to talk to Alfie.

She really didn't want to hear about it.

*****

She kept out of his way at college most of the day, but she couldn't help hearing some of the things that Joe and Adam were saying.

They kept on and on about it.

What had he done? What had she done?

To be fair, Alfie didn't seem to want to talk about it. It was just that the other two wouldn't stop.

Then some of the other boys joined in.

Carrie didn't go to college yet, so at least Jen didn't have to watch her and Alfie together.

But she wasn't jealous. No way.

It was just that he was her best friend and she didn't want to lose that.

She kept away for most of the week, but on Friday morning Alfie was waiting for her.

'I really need to talk,' he said.

THREE

Just Let Me Speak!

She wasn't sure she wanted to hear this.

'It's about me and Carrie.'

'I don't really want to know,' she said. 'I know what you've been doing. Everybody knows.'

'Yes, but … '

'Look, it's not down to me, but have you really thought about it?'

Jen was going to say what she thought. Then maybe Alfie wouldn't want to tell her anything else.

'She might get pregnant, or … '

'I'm not that stupid!' Alfie interrupted. 'That's not what I want to talk about.'

'And you know you're not the first.'

Jen was getting cross now, or she wouldn't have said anything.

'Joe and Adam said she … '

'Just let me speak, will you? I need you to listen.'

Alfie was yelling back now.

FOUR

I Can't Tell Them

Alfie had gone red in the face and looked really upset.

'We didn't do anything. OK?'

'But, at her party you ... '

'At her party she wanted to. And it was

her birthday and everything, so I went upstairs with her. But, in her mum's house, and with everyone downstairs, it wasn't right and I couldn't do it.'

'What did she say?'

'She was OK then, but she still wants to.'

'What about you?'

'I don't! She's saying there's something wrong with me, but it's not that. It just doesn't feel right.'

Jen didn't know what to say. But she knew one thing. She was happy.

'Can't you talk to Joe or Adam?'

'You must be joking! They think it's great. They keep going on, asking for all the dirt.'

'Well, what have you told them?'

Alfie went red in the face again. He looked at the floor.

'I can't tell them the truth, can I?'

FIVE

We'll Think of Something

'We've got to get to college,' said Jen. 'Let me think about it. We'll meet in the park later.'

She needed time. She had to help him

get out of the mess.

But how?

*****

It was early evening by the time they met up in the park.

Alfie looked really unhappy.

'We had a row,' he said. 'She says she'll dump me and tell everyone why. What am I going to do?'

He wiped his hand over his eyes. He was crying. Jen hadn't seen him cry for years.

She put her arms around him and pulled him close.

'Don't worry, we'll think of something.'

'Help me, Jen.'

She couldn't help herself. She kissed him.

He put his arms round her and kissed her back.

Suddenly he felt other arms round him.

Pulling him away!

'This explains everything! You cheat!'

It was Carrie.

'It was her you wanted all the time. You're dumped!'

She slapped Alfie's face, turned and walked away.

He turned back to Jen.

'You know something,' he said. 'She's right.'

Questions on the Story

- Why doesn't Carrie like Jen?

- Why does Jen tell Alfie that 'he's not the first' in Chapter Three?

- What did Alfie's friends think he had done?

Discussion Points

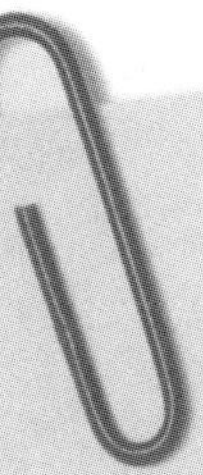

- Why didn't Alfie want to admit to his friends that he hadn't had sex with Carrie?

- Why was Jen happy (in Chapter Four)?

- Why had Alfie decided that he didn’t want to have sex?

Street Wise

Activities

- Write the conversation between Alfie, Joe and Adam. Alfie doesn't want to tell them what really happened.

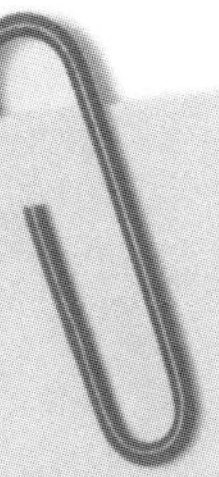

- Write Jen's diary, finishing with the kiss in the park and her thoughts about it.

- Research sexually transmitted diseases, and produce a leaflet.